PRINCEWILL LAGANG

Conflict Resolution for Couples

Contents

1

Introduction to Conflict Resolution for Couples

In any romantic relationship, conflicts are bound to arise. These conflicts can range from minor disagreements to more significant issues that challenge the foundation of the relationship. How these conflicts are managed and resolved can make a significant impact on the overall health and longevity of the relationship. This chapter will delve into the importance of effective conflict resolution in relationships and set the stage for exploring strategies to navigate conflicts constructively.

Section 1.1: The Significance of Effective Conflict Resolution

Conflict resolution is the process of addressing disagreements, misunderstandings, or differing opinions in a manner that is respectful, productive, and conducive to maintaining a healthy relationship. In the context of couples, conflict resolution becomes even more crucial, as it directly affects the emotional bond between partners. Unresolved conflicts can lead to resentment, communication breakdown, and, ultimately, the deterioration of the relationship.

This section will emphasize the following points:

1. Preservation of Emotional Connection: Conflicts, if not managed well, can erode the emotional connection between partners. Effective conflict resolution ensures that both individuals feel heard, understood, and valued, thereby preserving the emotional intimacy that drew them together.

2. Enhancement of Communication: Conflict resolution provides an opportunity for couples to improve their communication skills. It encourages active listening, empathy, and the ability to express feelings and needs in a constructive manner.

3. Prevention of Escalation: Unresolved conflicts tend to escalate over time, often leading to intense arguments and hurtful behavior. Learning how to resolve conflicts effectively helps prevent such escalation and its damaging consequences.

Section 1.2: Navigating Conflicts Constructively

Before delving into specific conflict resolution strategies, it's important to establish a foundation for constructive conflict navigation. This section will provide an overview of the mindset and approach that are conducive to resolving conflicts in a healthy way.

1. Openness to Differences: Partners should recognize that differences in opinions, values, and preferences are natural in any relationship. Rather than viewing these differences as obstacles, they should be seen as opportunities for growth and understanding.

2. Mutual Respect: Respect forms the cornerstone of effective conflict resolution. Both partners should commit to treating each other with kindness and consideration, even during disagreements.

3. Focus on Solutions, Not Winning: Conflict resolution is not about winning an argument, but rather finding a solution that meets both partners' needs. This mindset shift can help avoid a power struggle and promote collaboration.

4. Timing and Environment: Choosing an appropriate time and setting to address conflicts is crucial. Engaging in conflict resolution when both partners are calm and receptive, and in a private and comfortable environment, sets the stage for a productive conversation.

Section 1.3: Preview of Strategies

To wrap up the introduction, a brief preview of the conflict resolution strategies covered in subsequent chapters will be provided. These strategies will include active listening, "I" statements, finding common ground, compromise, seeking professional help when needed, and more.

Conclusion: Laying the Groundwork

In conclusion, effective conflict resolution is a vital skill for couples who seek a harmonious and enduring relationship. By recognizing its significance, adopting the right mindset, and embracing constructive approaches, couples can navigate conflicts in a way that strengthens their connection rather than weakening it. The following chapters will delve deeper into the practical strategies that couples can employ to manage conflicts and promote relationship well-being.

2

Understanding the Nature of Conflict

onflicts are an inevitable part of any relationship, and understanding their nature is essential for effective resolution. This chapter will explore the common causes and dynamics of conflicts in relationships, as well as the underlying issues that contribute to disagreements.

Section 2.1: Common Causes of Conflicts

1. Communication Breakdown: Miscommunication, misunderstandings, and poor listening skills can lead to conflicts. Partners may interpret messages differently, causing frustration and tension.

2. Unmet Needs: When individual needs for affection, attention, appreciation, or intimacy are not fulfilled, conflicts can arise. These unmet needs can manifest as emotional or behavioral issues.

3. Differences in Values and Beliefs: Conflicts often stem from differences in core values, religious beliefs, or life goals. Partners may have contrasting views on family, career, or lifestyle choices.

4. Expectations vs. Reality: Unfulfilled expectations can lead to disappointment and conflict. Partners may have differing assumptions about roles, responsibilities, or the course of the relationship.

5. Jealousy and Insecurity: Feelings of jealousy and insecurity can trigger conflicts. Trust issues, perceived threats, or comparisons to others can strain the relationship.

Section 2.2: Dynamics of Conflicts

1. Escalation: Conflicts can escalate when partners become emotionally charged and resort to blaming, shouting, or hurtful language. Escalation often makes it harder to reach a resolution.

2. Silent Treatment: Avoidance or the silent treatment can prolong conflicts. Ignoring the issue doesn't resolve it; instead, it fosters resentment and a lack of communication.

3. Negative Interpretation: Partners may interpret each other's actions negatively, assuming the worst intentions. This leads to misunderstandings and further conflict.

4. Unresolved Past Issues: Unresolved conflicts from the past can resurface and compound present disagreements. These unresolved issues can become a source of ongoing tension.

Section 2.3: Underlying Issues in Conflicts

1. Power Imbalance: Conflicts can arise when one partner exerts dominance or control over the other. Power struggles can manifest in various ways, such as decision-making or financial control.

2. Fear of Vulnerability: Unresolved conflicts can stem from a fear of being

vulnerable. Partners might avoid discussing their true feelings to protect themselves from potential hurt.

3. Lack of Emotional Intimacy: A lack of emotional connection can lead to conflicts. Partners may feel unheard or distant from each other, causing them to argue more frequently.

4. External Stressors: External factors like work stress, financial problems, or family issues can spill over into the relationship, intensifying conflicts.

Conclusion: Insights into Conflict Dynamics

Understanding the underlying causes and dynamics of conflicts is essential for addressing them effectively. By recognizing the sources of disagreements and acknowledging the emotions and vulnerabilities involved, couples can begin to work towards resolutions that promote understanding, compromise, and growth. The following chapters will delve into specific strategies to tackle these conflicts head-on and build stronger, more resilient relationships.

3

The Role of Communication in Conflict Resolution

Communication is the cornerstone of effective conflict resolution in relationships. This chapter explores the vital connection between communication and resolving conflicts, along with techniques to foster open dialogue and active listening.

Section 3.1: The Crucial Connection between Communication and Conflict Resolution

Communication serves as the bridge through which partners express their feelings, needs, and perspectives. When conflicts arise, clear and empathetic communication is essential to prevent misunderstandings from escalating into larger issues. This section highlights the significance of communication in the conflict resolution process:

1. Expression of Emotions: Open communication allows partners to express their emotions, helping them understand each other's feelings and experiences.

2. Clarification of Misunderstandings: Misinterpretations can easily lead to conflicts. Effective communication helps clarify intentions and prevent unnecessary disagreements.

3. Conflict De-Escalation: By fostering open dialogue, partners can discuss issues calmly and work towards resolving conflicts before they escalate.

Section 3.2: Techniques for Fostering Open Dialogue

1. Use of "I" Statements: Encourage the use of "I" statements instead of accusatory "you" statements. This approach focuses on expressing personal feelings and experiences rather than blaming the other person.

2. Timing and Setting: Choose an appropriate time and setting for discussions. Avoid addressing conflicts when one or both partners are already stressed or distracted.

3. Stay Calm and Respectful: Maintain a calm tone and respectful demeanor, even if emotions are running high. This helps create a safe environment for open communication.

Section 3.3: Techniques for Active Listening

1. Give Full Attention: When your partner is speaking, give them your full attention. Put away distractions and focus on what they're saying.

2. Empathetic Responses: Show empathy by acknowledging your partner's feelings and validating their perspective. This helps them feel heard and understood.

3. Ask Clarifying Questions: If something is unclear, ask questions for clarification. This demonstrates your interest in truly understanding their point of view.

4. Summarize and Reflect: Summarize what your partner has said and reflect it back to them. This ensures you're on the same page and helps prevent misinterpretations.

Section 3.4: Active Listening vs. Passive Listening

Active listening involves fully engaging in the conversation, while passive listening is a more superficial form of hearing. Active listening requires effort and intention, but it's crucial for effective conflict resolution:

1. Engagement: Active listening shows your partner that you value their thoughts and feelings, fostering a sense of connection.

2. Preventing Assumptions: Passive listening can lead to assumptions and misunderstandings. Active listening helps clarify meanings and intentions.

Conclusion: Communication as the Key

Effective communication is the foundation upon which successful conflict resolution is built. By fostering open dialogue, using active listening techniques, and prioritizing understanding and empathy, couples can navigate conflicts in a way that promotes connection and resolution. In the next chapters, we will explore additional strategies that complement effective communication and contribute to a harmonious relationship.

4

Strategies for Calming the Storm

Conflicts can often be emotionally charged and intense. This chapter focuses on approaches to de-escalating conflicts, managing emotional intensity, and creating a safe environment for discussing sensitive topics.

Section 4.1: De-Escalating Conflicts

1. Take a Break: If a conflict becomes heated, take a break to cool off. This pause allows emotions to settle and prevents the situation from spiraling out of control.

2. Use Humor: A well-timed, light-hearted comment can defuse tension and shift the focus away from negativity.

3. Practice Deep Breathing: Deep breathing exercises help reduce stress and can be used during conflicts to stay calm and composed.

Section 4.2: Managing Emotional Intensity

1. Express Emotions Calmly: Share your emotions without shouting or blaming. Using a calm tone and respectful language can prevent the escalation of conflicts.

2. Acknowledge Emotions: Validate each other's emotions. Letting your partner know that their feelings are understood can help diffuse emotional tension.

3. Focus on the Issue, Not Each Other: Instead of attacking each other personally, focus on the specific issue at hand. This prevents the conflict from becoming personal.

Section 4.3: Creating a Safe Environment

1. Use "We" Language: Frame the discussion as a joint effort by using "we" language. This conveys that you're both in this together, working towards resolution.

2. Agree on Ground Rules: Establish rules for communication, such as no yelling, interrupting, or name-calling. This creates a safe space for discussing conflicts.

3. Be Vulnerable: Share your feelings and vulnerabilities. This encourages your partner to do the same and promotes empathy and understanding.

Section 4.4: Active Problem-Solving

1. Identify Core Issues: Pinpoint the underlying issues causing the conflict. Often, conflicts are symptoms of deeper concerns.

2. Brainstorm Solutions: Collaborate on potential solutions to the problem. Focus on finding a resolution that benefits both partners.

3. Seek Compromise: Be willing to meet in the middle. Compromise doesn't mean giving up your needs entirely, but finding a solution that satisfies both parties.

Conclusion: Navigating Stormy Waters

In times of conflict, it's essential to approach the situation with a calm demeanor and a willingness to engage constructively. By de-escalating conflicts, managing emotional intensity, and creating a safe environment for discussion, couples can navigate through even the stormiest of situations. Employing these strategies sets the stage for productive conversations and effective conflict resolution. In the next chapter, we'll explore ways to rebuild trust and strengthen the emotional connection after conflicts have been resolved.

Seeking Understanding Through Empathy

Empathy plays a pivotal role in conflict resolution, allowing couples to connect on a deeper level and find common ground. This chapter delves into how empathy enhances conflict resolution and provides strategies for understanding and validating each other's perspectives.

Section 5.1: The Power of Empathy in Conflict Resolution

1. Creating Emotional Connection: Empathy bridges the gap between partners by fostering emotional connection and understanding.

2. Reducing Defensiveness: When partners feel understood, they are less likely to become defensive or resistant during conflicts.

3. Promoting Cooperation: Empathy encourages collaboration and cooperation, enabling partners to work together towards a solution.

Section 5.2: Strategies for Practicing Empathy

1. Active Listening: Give your full attention and show genuine interest in

your partner's feelings and thoughts. Make eye contact, nod, and respond appropriately.

2. Reflective Responses: Reflect back what your partner is saying to show that you understand. Use phrases like, "I hear you saying that you feel..."

3. Ask Open-Ended Questions: Pose open-ended questions to encourage your partner to share more about their feelings and perspective.

4. Validate Emotions: Acknowledge your partner's feelings without judgment. Validating emotions shows that you respect their point of view.

Section 5.3: Practicing Perspective-Taking

1. Put Yourself in Their Shoes: Imagine the situation from your partner's perspective. Consider how they might be feeling and why.

2. Recognize Your Own Biases: Be aware of your own biases and assumptions that might color your perception of the conflict.

3. Ask for Clarification: If you're unsure about your partner's perspective, ask questions to gain a clearer understanding of their thoughts and emotions.

Section 5.4: Validating Each Other's Perspectives

1. Avoid Dismissing Feelings: Even if you don't agree with your partner's viewpoint, avoid dismissing their feelings as unimportant or invalid.

2. Express Understanding: Use statements like, "I can see why you might feel that way," to show that you acknowledge their perspective.

3. Find Common Ground: Identify areas of agreement or shared experiences to build a foundation for resolution.

Conclusion: Building Bridges of Understanding

Empathy is a bridge that connects partners, enabling them to truly understand each other's feelings and experiences. By practicing active listening, perspective-taking, and validating each other's perspectives, couples can create an environment of mutual understanding, even during conflicts. The ability to empathize forms the basis for effective conflict resolution and strengthens the emotional bond between partners. In the next chapter, we will explore the importance of forgiveness in moving forward after conflicts.

6

Navigating Differences and Finding Common Ground

In conflicts, the ability to find compromises and common ground is essential for reaching resolutions that satisfy both partners. This chapter focuses on techniques for navigating differences and achieving win-win outcomes in conflicts.

Section 6.1: The Importance of Compromise

1. Preserving the Relationship: Compromise prevents conflicts from damaging the relationship by showing that both partners' needs are valued.

2. Balancing Needs: Compromising involves finding a middle ground where both partners' needs are met to some extent.

Section 6.2: Strategies for Finding Compromises

1. Identify Shared Goals: Find common goals that you both share, and work together towards achieving them.

2. List Priorities: Create a list of priorities for each partner, then find ways to address those priorities in a balanced manner.

3. Trade-Offs: Identify areas where you can give up something less important to you in exchange for something important to your partner.

Section 6.3: The Art of Win-Win Negotiation

1. Separate Interests from Positions: Dig deeper to understand the underlying interests behind each partner's position. This opens up more possibilities for compromise.

2. Brainstorm Multiple Options: Encourage creative thinking by generating multiple solutions to the conflict. This widens the scope for finding common ground.

3. Evaluate and Decide: Analyze the proposed solutions together. Determine which one best meets both partners' needs and objectives.

Section 6.4: Communicating During Compromise

1. Use "And" Instead of "But": Replace "but" with "and" to show that you're considering both perspectives, rather than dismissing one.

2. Focus on Solutions: Keep the conversation centered on finding solutions, rather than dwelling on the problems.

Section 6.5: Avoiding a Win-Lose Mentality

1. Collaborative Mindset: Approach conflicts with the intention of finding a solution that benefits both partners, rather than aiming to "win" at the other's expense.

2. Consider Long-Term Effects: Winning an argument in the short term might lead to resentment and further conflicts in the long run.

Conclusion: Sailing Towards Common Ground

Navigating differences and finding common ground requires a combination of compromise, negotiation, and a collaborative mindset. By focusing on shared goals, brainstorming multiple options, and practicing effective communication, couples can work together to achieve resolutions that satisfy both partners. The art of win-win negotiation not only resolves conflicts but also strengthens the foundation of the relationship. In the final chapter, we will explore the significance of forgiveness and moving forward after conflicts have been resolved.

7

Healthy Ways to Express Anger and Disagreement

Anger and disagreements are natural parts of any relationship. This chapter delves into the significance of expressing anger constructively and provides strategies for managing anger and disagreements in a healthy manner.

Section 7.1: The Importance of Constructive Expression

1. Preventing Resentment: Expressing anger in a healthy way prevents it from festering and turning into long-term resentment.

2. Maintaining Communication: Constructive expression of anger allows partners to continue communicating even during disagreements.

Section 7.2: Strategies for Managing Anger

1. Practice Self-Awareness: Recognize your triggers and patterns of anger. This self-awareness helps you manage your reactions.

2. Take a Break: If you're feeling overwhelmed with anger, step away from the situation to cool off before discussing it.

3. Use "I" Statements: Express your feelings using "I" statements to communicate how the situation has affected you.

4. Avoid Blame and Accusation: Focus on the specific issue rather than blaming or accusing your partner.

Section 7.3: Techniques for Healthy Disagreements

1. Stay Calm: Keep your emotions in check during disagreements. Reacting emotionally can escalate conflicts.

2. Listen Actively: Listen to your partner's perspective without interrupting or planning your response.

3. Find Common Ground: Identify areas of agreement to build upon and use them as a foundation for resolution.

Section 7.4: The Role of Empathy in Angry Moments

1. Understand Triggers: Empathize with each other's triggers and understand why certain issues evoke strong emotions.

2. Validate Emotions: Acknowledge your partner's feelings even if you don't agree with them. Validation defuses defensiveness.

Section 7.5: Revisiting Solutions

1. Revisit Discussions: If a solution isn't working as expected, revisit the discussion and make adjustments.

2. Learn from Conflict: Use conflicts as opportunities to learn about each other and refine your communication and conflict resolution skills.

Conclusion: Taming the Fire of Conflict

Expressing anger and managing disagreements constructively is essential for maintaining a healthy relationship. By recognizing the importance of healthy expression, practicing self-awareness, and communicating with empathy, couples can navigate anger and disagreements without causing lasting damage. Employing these strategies helps keep the fire of conflict contained and ensures that disagreements don't consume the relationship. In the final chapter, we'll explore the role of forgiveness in healing and moving forward after conflicts.

8

Managing Conflict Styles and Patterns

Individuals bring distinct conflict styles and patterns to their relationships. This chapter examines the identification of these styles and patterns, and offers strategies to adapt and balance them for more effective conflict resolution.

Section 8.1: Understanding Individual Conflict Styles

1. Avoidance: Some individuals tend to avoid conflicts altogether, hoping they will resolve on their own.

2. Accommodation: This style involves prioritizing the needs and desires of the partner over one's own.

3. Competition: Competitive individuals assert their viewpoints strongly and may be less willing to compromise.

4. Compromise: This style seeks middle ground and involves some level of give-and-take.

5. Collaboration: Collaborators aim for win-win solutions and value both their needs and their partner's.

Section 8.2: Recognizing Patterns

1. Frequency: Observe how often conflicts arise and whether they follow certain triggers or events.

2. Responses: Note common responses during conflicts, such as withdrawal, anger, or passive-aggressiveness.

3. Resolution: Pay attention to how conflicts are typically resolved—whether they lead to compromise, avoidance, or escalated arguments.

Section 8.3: Adapting Conflict Styles for Effective Resolution

1. Open Dialogue: Encourage open discussions about each other's preferred conflict styles. Understand where they come from and how they impact conflicts.

2. Assessing Effectiveness: Reflect on which conflict styles have been effective in the past and which have led to negative outcomes.

3. Balancing Styles: Aim to balance styles for better resolution. For instance, a competitive partner can learn to compromise, and an avoidant partner can practice more open communication.

Section 8.4: Embracing Flexibility

1. Recognize Context: Different situations may call for different conflict styles. Adapt based on the context of the conflict.

2. Practice Empathy: Understand why your partner employs a certain style.

This helps you appreciate their perspective.

3. Negotiate Win-Win Solutions: Aim for collaboration whenever possible to reach solutions that satisfy both partners.

Section 8.5: Seeking Professional Guidance

1. Counseling: If conflicting styles and patterns lead to persistent issues, seeking the guidance of a professional can be beneficial.

2. Mediation: A mediator can help couples navigate conflicts and find resolutions in a neutral environment.

Conclusion: Crafting a Balanced Approach

Understanding and managing conflict styles and patterns is vital for effective resolution. By recognizing your own and your partner's styles, adapting them based on the situation, and seeking balance and compromise, you can create a more harmonious conflict resolution process. This chapter marks the final step in building comprehensive conflict resolution skills. In the next chapter, we'll explore the concept of forgiveness and its role in healing relationships after conflicts.

9

Constructive Conflict: A Pathway to Growth

Conflicts, often seen as disruptive, can actually be pathways to personal and relational growth. This chapter delves into understanding the potential for growth through conflicts and provides techniques for viewing them as opportunities for positive change.

Section 9.1: Recognizing the Potential for Growth

1. Increased Understanding: Conflicts reveal differing perspectives and feelings, enhancing understanding between partners.

2. Problem-Solving Skills: Navigating conflicts fosters the development of effective problem-solving skills.

3. Improved Communication: Learning to express needs and listen actively during conflicts enhances overall communication.

Section 9.2: Shifting Perspectives on Conflicts

1. Seeing Challenges as Opportunities: View conflicts as chances to address issues and strengthen the relationship.

2. Learning from Disagreements: Conflicts offer insights into each partner's triggers, needs, and preferences, promoting personal growth.

Section 9.3: Techniques for Positive Change

1. Reflect on Patterns: Analyze recurring conflicts to identify patterns and underlying issues. This awareness opens doors to growth.

2. Set Growth Goals: Collaboratively set goals for personal and relational growth that arise from conflict resolution.

3. Practice Self-Compassion: Be kind to yourself when conflicts arise. Recognize that growth involves learning from mistakes.

Section 9.4: Cultivating Empathy and Perspective-Taking

1. Empathetic Reflection: Put yourself in your partner's shoes to understand their feelings and viewpoints.

2. Seeing Through Their Lens: Understand how conflicts affect your partner personally, and consider their emotional experiences.

Section 9.5: Practicing Forgiveness and Healing

1. Letting Go of Resentment: Forgiveness allows both partners to move forward without carrying the weight of past conflicts.

2. Healing Together: The process of forgiving and healing deepens the emotional connection between partners.

Conclusion: Embracing the Growth Within Conflict

Embracing conflicts as opportunities for growth transforms the way we approach disagreements. By recognizing the potential for enhanced understanding, improved communication, and personal development, couples can navigate conflicts with a positive mindset. Shifting perspectives, cultivating empathy, and practicing forgiveness pave the way for a stronger and more resilient relationship. This chapter marks the conclusion of our journey through conflict resolution. Remember that every conflict holds the potential for positive change.

10

Rebuilding Trust and Connection After Conflict

After conflicts, rebuilding trust and reconnecting emotionally are crucial for maintaining a healthy relationship. This chapter explores strategies for navigating the aftermath of conflicts and restoring trust and emotional bonds.

Section 10.1: Acknowledging the Aftermath

1. Emotional Impact: Recognize the emotional toll that conflicts can have on both partners.

2. Residual Tension: Understand that conflicts can leave residual tension that needs addressing.

Section 10.2: Strategies for Restoring Trust

1. Open Communication: Engage in honest discussions about the conflict, addressing its impact on trust.

2. Apologize and Forgive: Apologize for any hurtful actions or words, and offer forgiveness to your partner as well.

3. Consistency: Consistently act in ways that reinforce your commitment to the relationship and rebuild trust.

Section 10.3: Rebuilding Emotional Bonds

1. Quality Time: Spend quality time together to nurture emotional closeness.

2. Express Appreciation: Regularly express gratitude and appreciation for your partner.

3. Shared Activities: Engage in activities you both enjoy to foster shared experiences.

Section 10.4: Learning from Conflicts

1. Reflect on Lessons: Discuss the lessons learned from conflicts and how they can contribute to growth.

2. Communication Improvements: Implement communication strategies developed during conflict resolution.

Section 10.5: Seeking Professional Help

1. Therapy: If rebuilding trust and connection proves challenging, seek the help of a therapist to facilitate the process.

2. Counseling: Couples counseling can offer guidance in rebuilding emotional bonds and trust.

Conclusion: Renewed Trust, Stronger Bonds

The aftermath of conflicts provides an opportunity to rebuild trust and emotional connection, often resulting in a stronger relationship. By addressing the emotional impact of conflicts, implementing strategies for rebuilding trust and fostering emotional closeness, couples can navigate the post-conflict phase with intention and dedication. This chapter concludes our exploration of conflict resolution and highlights the significance of the journey towards healing and growth.

11

Avoiding Destructive Patterns: Red Flags and Solutions

Destructive conflict patterns can erode the foundation of a relationship. This chapter focuses on identifying such patterns, understanding their impact, and providing techniques for breaking unhealthy cycles and adopting more constructive behaviors.

Section 11.1: Recognizing Destructive Conflict Patterns

1. Constant Criticism: Habitually criticizing your partner's actions, character, or choices.

2. Stonewalling: Withdrawing or shutting down during conflicts, avoiding discussions altogether.

3. Defensiveness: Always being on the defensive, not considering your partner's perspective.

4. Escalation: Allowing conflicts to spiral out of control with escalating

arguments.

Section 11.2: Understanding Their Impact

1. Communication Breakdown: Destructive patterns hinder healthy communication and conflict resolution.

2. Emotional Distance: These patterns lead to emotional disconnection and detachment between partners.

3. Resentment: Unresolved conflicts stemming from these patterns foster resentment and negativity.

Section 11.3: Techniques for Breaking Unhealthy Cycles

1. Self-Awareness: Recognize when you're engaging in destructive patterns and commit to changing them.

2. Practice Mindfulness: Develop mindfulness techniques to stay present during conflicts and avoid automatic negative reactions.

3. Time-Outs: If conflict escalates, take a time-out to cool off and prevent further damage.

Section 11.4: Adopting Constructive Behaviors

1. Use "I" Statements: Express your feelings and needs using "I" statements instead of blaming your partner.

2. Active Listening: Listen attentively without interrupting, demonstrating your willingness to understand.

3. Accept Influence: Be open to considering your partner's perspective and

adapting your stance.

Section 11.5: Seeking Professional Help

1. Therapeutic Intervention: If destructive patterns persist, consider seeking the assistance of a therapist.

2. Counseling: Couples counseling can help you both learn healthier ways of addressing conflicts.

Conclusion: Building a Foundation of Healthy Patterns

Avoiding destructive conflict patterns is essential for maintaining a healthy relationship. By recognizing these patterns, understanding their impact, and adopting constructive behaviors, couples can build a foundation of open communication, empathy, and collaboration. This chapter marks the importance of consciously working towards healthier dynamics, ensuring that conflicts do not undermine the relationship's well-being.

12

The Ongoing Journey of Conflict Resolution

Conflict resolution isn't a destination but an ongoing journey in relationships. This chapter reflects on the continuous nature of conflict resolution and provides insights into nurturing a culture of ongoing growth, communication, and harmony.

Section 12.1: Embracing Conflict as a Part of Life

1. Inevitability of Conflicts: Understand that conflicts are a natural aspect of any relationship and should not be feared.

2. Opportunities for Growth: Embrace conflicts as opportunities to learn, adapt, and grow both individually and as a couple.

Section 12.2: Cultivating Open Communication

1. Regular Check-Ins: Engage in regular conversations to discuss how each partner is feeling about the relationship and any potential conflicts.

2. Safe Environment: Create a safe space where both partners can openly share their thoughts and emotions without fear of judgment.

Section 12.3: Adapting Conflict Resolution Strategies

1. Evolving Together: As individuals and circumstances change, be willing to adapt and evolve your conflict resolution strategies.

2. Learning from Mistakes: View conflicts as learning opportunities, and assess what worked and what didn't in previous resolutions.

Section 12.4: Celebrating Progress

1. Acknowledge Efforts: Celebrate the progress you've made in handling conflicts constructively.

2. Reward Growth: Reward yourselves for implementing positive changes and growing together.

Section 12.5: Seeking Professional Guidance

1. Regular Check-Ins with a Therapist: Consider periodic check-ins with a therapist to ensure you're on track and addressing any recurring issues.

2. Refresher Counseling: Participate in counseling sessions to fine-tune your conflict resolution skills and reinforce positive behaviors.

Conclusion: Nurturing a Culture of Growth and Harmony

Conflict resolution is not a one-time task but an ongoing commitment to growth and harmony. By embracing conflicts as opportunities, nurturing open communication, and adapting your strategies over time, couples can create a culture of continuous improvement and a strong foundation for their relationship. This chapter marks the conclusion of our exploration of conflict resolution, underlining the importance of investing in the ongoing journey of building a thriving partnership.

36

www.ingramcontent.com/pod-product-compliance
Lightning Source LLC
Chambersburg PA
CBHW061320140726
47998CB00006B/2484